DAEDALUS
and ICARUS

DAEDALUS
and ICARUS

Penelope Farmer
Illustrated by Chris Connor

Harcourt Brace Jovanovich, Inc., New York

© Text Penelope Farmer 1971
© Illustrations Chris Connor 1971

First American edition 1971
Originally published in Great Britain by William Collins Sons & Co. Ltd
Hardbound edition ISBN 0-15-221212-4
Library edition ISBN 0-15-221213-2
Library of Congress Catalog Card Number: 71-96318
Printed in Great Britain

The sun ruled the sky above the island. The sea licked about its shores, catching the light and glittering. The land absorbed the brightness of the sun, but the sun and sea seemed to talk together.

The sea was the Aegean, of gods and heroes, the island Crete.

To Crete across the sea there fled a man called Daedalus. He was an engineer, the most brilliant inventor of his time and no one more aware of that than he. Indeed his pride had led to this present flight; for when the skill of his nephew Talos had come near to rivalling his own, jealous Daedalus had pushed him from a rooftop to his death and, as punishment, had been exiled from Athens, city of his birth. He took with him into exile his young son Icarus. He idolized this boy. To hear him talk, you might think he'd invented him, not merely fathered him.

On Crete at Cnossus stood a palace, brilliant in the sun. Striped pillars supported it, and no one could have counted all its chambers, courts and halls. In the greatest of them sat Minos, King of Crete, on a throne inlaid with gold. He was mighty, a sun among other kings, ruling an empire of subject states all round the Aegean Sea. Before him even proud Daedalus came bowing low.

"Welcome, Daedalus, welcome to our court, O subtle engineer! Your name is known to us; we have heard also of your skill, which makes you doubly welcome here: for we have a task to meet such skill as yours. Indeed its accomplishment is the price of our hospitality to yourself and to your son."

Minos rose from his throne, led Daedalus and Icarus to a door set with iron bars. From the room beyond came a warmth, a stench like a farmyard.

"We desire you to build us a stronghold beneath our house from which nothing, from which no one can escape, neither man nor monster, not even monsters so mighty, so awful as this; for see, O Daedalus, our son, the Minotaur."

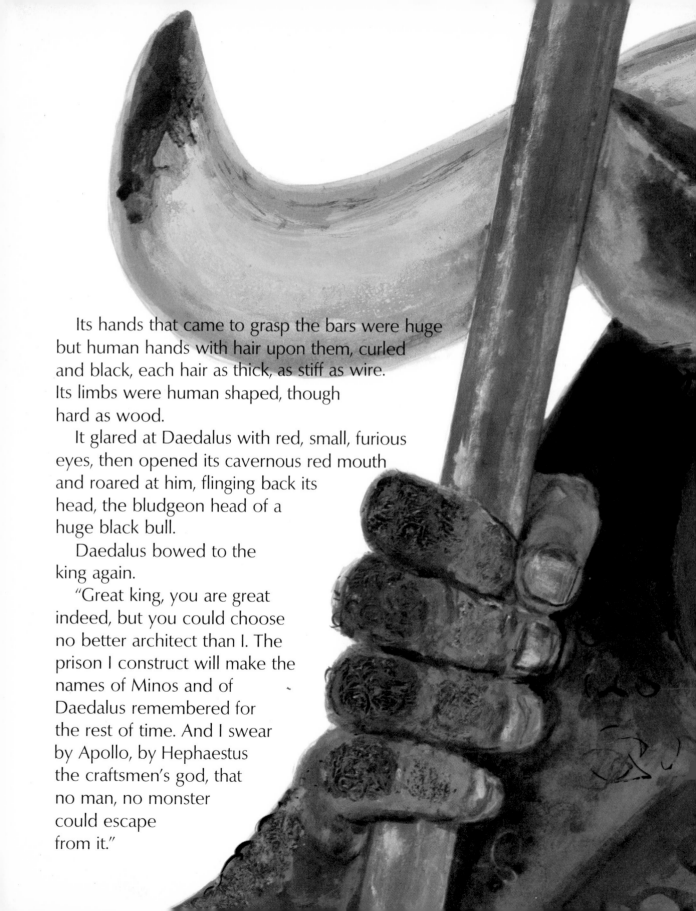

Its hands that came to grasp the bars were huge but human hands with hair upon them, curled and black, each hair as thick, as stiff as wire. Its limbs were human shaped, though hard as wood.

It glared at Daedalus with red, small, furious eyes, then opened its cavernous red mouth and roared at him, flinging back its head, the bludgeon head of a huge black bull.

Daedalus bowed to the king again.

"Great king, you are great indeed, but you could choose no better architect than I. The prison I construct will make the names of Minos and of Daedalus remembered for the rest of time. And I swear by Apollo, by Hephaestus the craftsmen's god, that no man, no monster could escape from it."

Daedalus drew plans first, scratching them out on tablets of yellow wax, plans too complex for any to decipher but himself. Then he set troops of slaves and laborers to work, enough men to make an army. Deep beneath the palace with picks and spades and hammers, they gouged out the rocks of Crete. Some hacked and smashed at them till

the sparks flew off. Some carried the rubble away in baskets on their backs; yet others cut props and pillars to support the roof.

Little by little they tunnelled from the bitter rock a labyrinth, a maze, an intricate confusion of tunnels and passages, with so many false turnings and alleyways that a hundred men could have wandered there or a hundred rivers flowed and neither man nor river ever met another.

In the labyrinth then lived the Minotaur, its roar confined in rock still heard dimly through the palace. People trembled hearing it. Minos, they knew, sent those who had angered him to feed his son, and to the Minotaur all alike were men of tender flesh to tear and devour—Cretan, Spartan, Athenian, none could withstand its furious charge from some dark winding of the labyrinth.

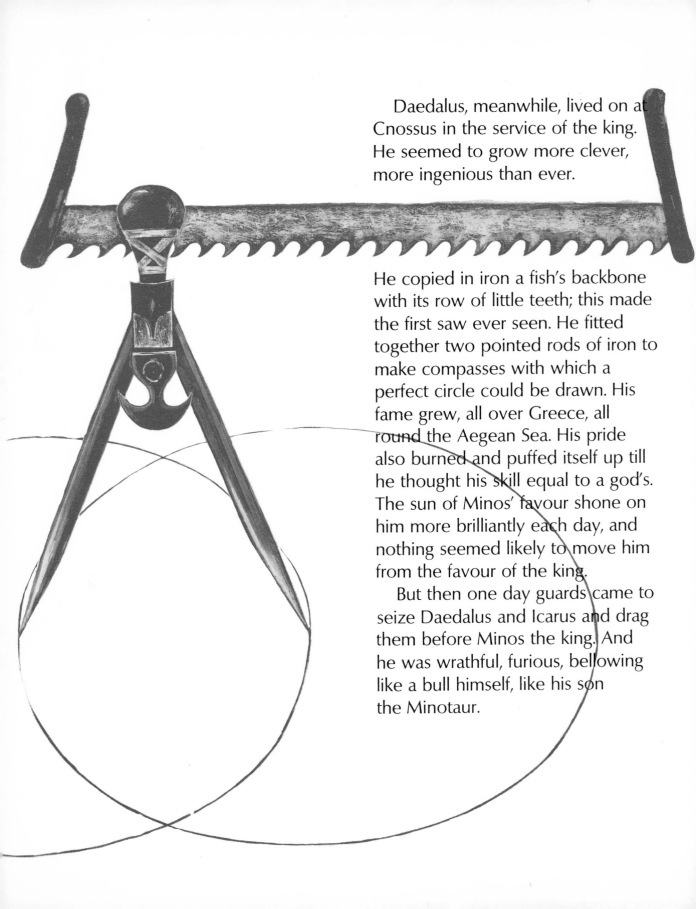

Daedalus, meanwhile, lived on at Cnossus in the service of the king. He seemed to grow more clever, more ingenious than ever.

He copied in iron a fish's backbone with its row of little teeth; this made the first saw ever seen. He fitted together two pointed rods of iron to make compasses with which a perfect circle could be drawn. His fame grew, all over Greece, all round the Aegean Sea. His pride also burned and puffed itself up till he thought his skill equal to a god's. The sun of Minos' favour shone on him more brilliantly each day, and nothing seemed likely to move him from the favour of the king.

But then one day guards came to seize Daedalus and Icarus and drag them before Minos the king. And he was wrathful, furious, bellowing like a bull himself, like his son the Minotaur.

"So you boasted, Daedalus, that no one could escape your labyrinth. But the Minotaur is dead. A man has killed our son and understood the maze and sailed away unharmed from Crete. Now you and your son shall be cast into the maze, and if you too escape from there, you'll get no further, we swear to it. We, Minos, do not swear in vain. We rule not merely Crete but all the sea about. Without ships no man can escape from Crete, and you, O subtle architect, clever as you are, you command no ships upon our Aegean Sea."

So Daedalus, with Icarus his son, was cast into the prison he had made. He took with him there a ball of golden thread, which looked in such darkness like an image of the golden sun. This was the device he'd made secretly to guide himself to the far end of the labyrinth. He tied one end to the entrance place, and slowly the ball began to unroll ahead of them, through all the turns and windings, the confusions of entrances and alleyways. After a while Daedalus smelt a familiar, farmyard reek, but it had a fouler, sicklier note to it, and the stench went on growing all the time till they reached the cave at the heart of the labyrinth where the corpse of the Minotaur lay rotting on dirty straw.

It seemed feeble now, and foolish and puny. Its red eyes were closed, its limbs flaccid and limp. Only the yellow horns still looked dangerous. Daedalus gazed beyond it, shuddering, holding up his little lamp till its light reached the farthest corners of the cave, where human bones and skulls lay scattered everywhere. There were feathers also from birds devoured by the Minotaur. He picked up one and examined minutely its shaft and quill.

"Minos rules the land of Crete," he said. "He may rule the sea that surrounds it too. But remember, Icarus my son, remember that great King Minos does not rule the sky."

Icarus did not know what his father meant by this. He watched Daedalus lay feathers overlapping in four separate rows, each diminishing in size from one end to the other. Then Daedalus brought from his tunic a cake of wax, a needle, and some fine strong thread. He joined the larger feathers with the needle and thread. He softened the wax in the warmth of the lamp and used it to unite the smaller feathers.

Icarus watched his father's patient hands, watched small feathers waver in the heat above the lamp and the wax drip down in slow, dull drops. Sometimes Daedalus made him hold feathers or pull on an end of thread, and he was eager to help, too eager perhaps, jogging his father's arm or letting his shadow fall across the light.

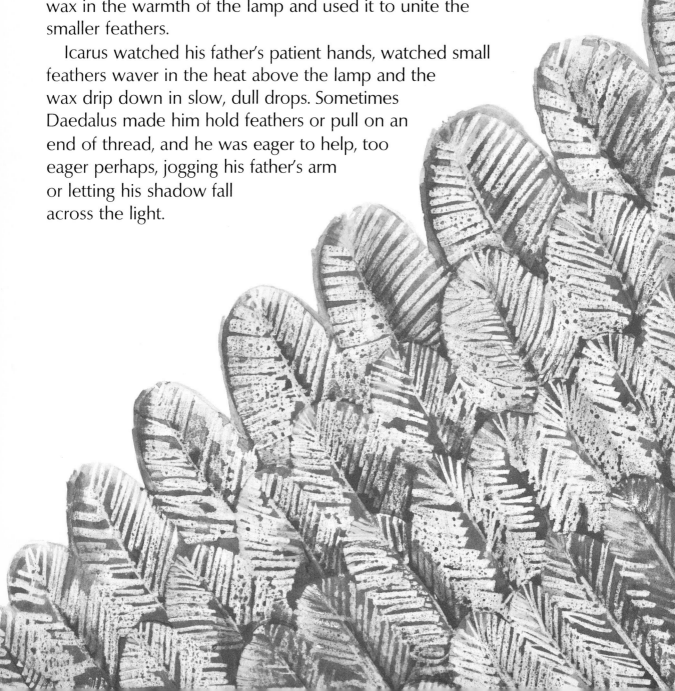

At last Daedalus took the completed rows, bent them and curved them into shape, and then his son could see what they were meant to be; how from the wings of birds, his father Daedalus had made wings for men, one pair each for himself and Icarus.

The oil of the lamp was all burned by now. As they left the cave the wick flickered and went out so that their only light was in the guiding thread, in the diminishing golden ball, which unrolled ahead of them towards the secret entrance of the labyrinth where no guards would stand in wait. The sound of their breathing magnified itself. On and on they went. Even when they neared the end, there was still no light, not the narrowest rim or chink. The thread doubled round and back again, and they twisted confusedly to follow it.

The light broke suddenly, burst upon them. They had to bury their eyes against the blinding, burning sun. The air rushed at them too, strong air full of honey and wild thyme, for this entrance to the labyrinth lay on the hillside by Cnossus, within sight of the glittering sea.

When Daedalus' eyes accepted light at last, he took some leather thongs and fixed the smaller pair of wings to the arms of Icarus. He fixed the larger to his own, explaining all the while what they had to do. They would have to use their arms just as the wing bones of a bird, making the feathers gently rise and fall.

"But mind, mind, Icarus my son, don't fly too low, too near the sea, for the feathers once wet will not carry you. But then do not fly too high, too near the sun, for the sun's heat like the lamp's, will melt the wax, make the feathers fall away."

Icarus heard his father out. But he was already impatient to begin, moving his arms experimentally, so that the air caught the feathers on the wings.

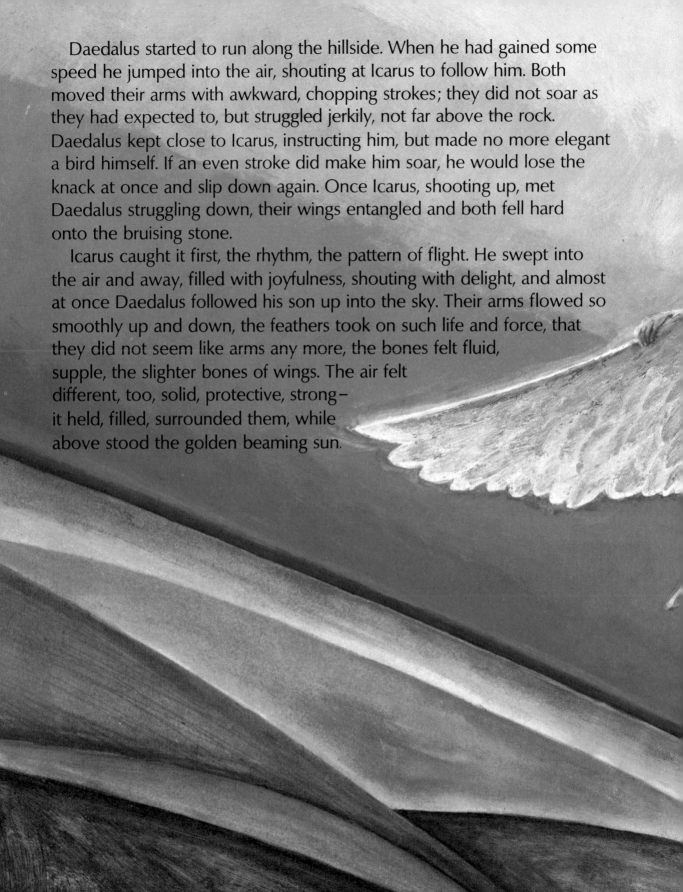

Daedalus started to run along the hillside. When he had gained some speed he jumped into the air, shouting at Icarus to follow him. Both moved their arms with awkward, chopping strokes; they did not soar as they had expected to, but struggled jerkily, not far above the rock. Daedalus kept close to Icarus, instructing him, but made no more elegant a bird himself. If an even stroke did make him soar, he would lose the knack at once and slip down again. Once Icarus, shooting up, met Daedalus struggling down, their wings entangled and both fell hard onto the bruising stone.

Icarus caught it first, the rhythm, the pattern of flight. He swept into the air and away, filled with joyfulness, shouting with delight, and almost at once Daedalus followed his son up into the sky. Their arms flowed so smoothly up and down, the feathers took on such life and force, that they did not seem like arms any more, the bones felt fluid, supple, the slighter bones of wings. The air felt different, too, solid, protective, strong – it held, filled, surrounded them, while above stood the golden beaming sun.

Higher and higher flew Daedalus and Icarus. Down below on land men began to notice them. Farmers leaned on their plows and looked up into the sky, shading their eyes against the sun. Washerwomen dropped the clothes they scrubbed, fishermen let fall their nets, boat-builders laid down the saws that Daedalus had made. When they began to fly across the sea, sailors came running to the sides of ships to stare at them. All imagined they saw gods not men.

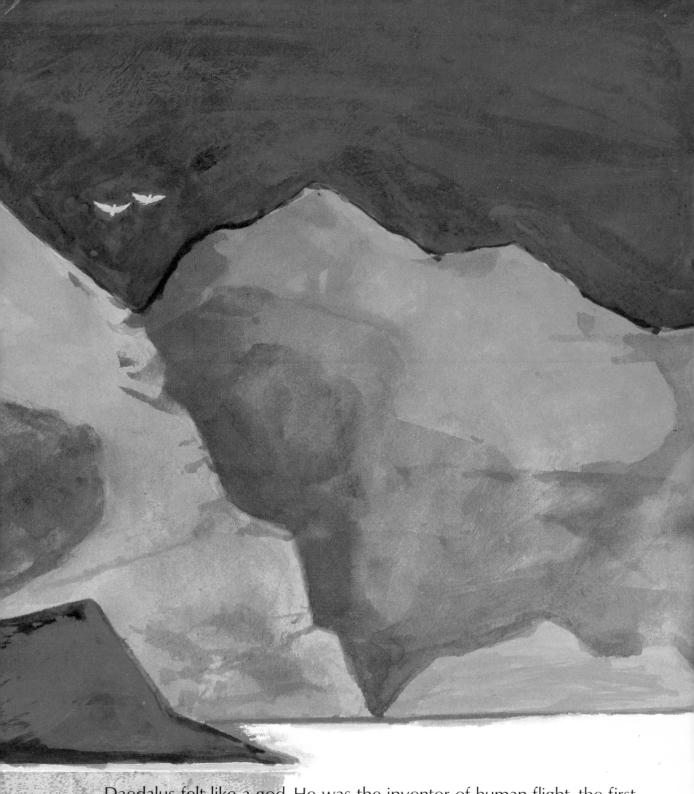

Daedalus felt like a god. He was the inventor of human flight, the first mortal man to fly. He shouted to the air, the sun, the sea, exultantly.
"What say you mighty gods? You have changed men into birds to make them fly. Icarus remains a boy yet flies like an eagle through the air."

Icarus flew more like a gull than an eagle now, skimming low, delightfully, across the shimmer of sea so that his father had to shout and wave to him to keep the feathers dry. Then Icarus left the sea and flew higher in the air. Though annoyed at first to be taken from his game he was soon seized by still greater joy, moving his arms in more and more powerful strokes, swooping, soaring upwards in the sky like the eagle his father imagined him.

Daedalus returned to his godlike dreams and failed to watch the flight of Icarus.

"Other men need gods to make them fly. Icarus has only his mortal father Daedalus."

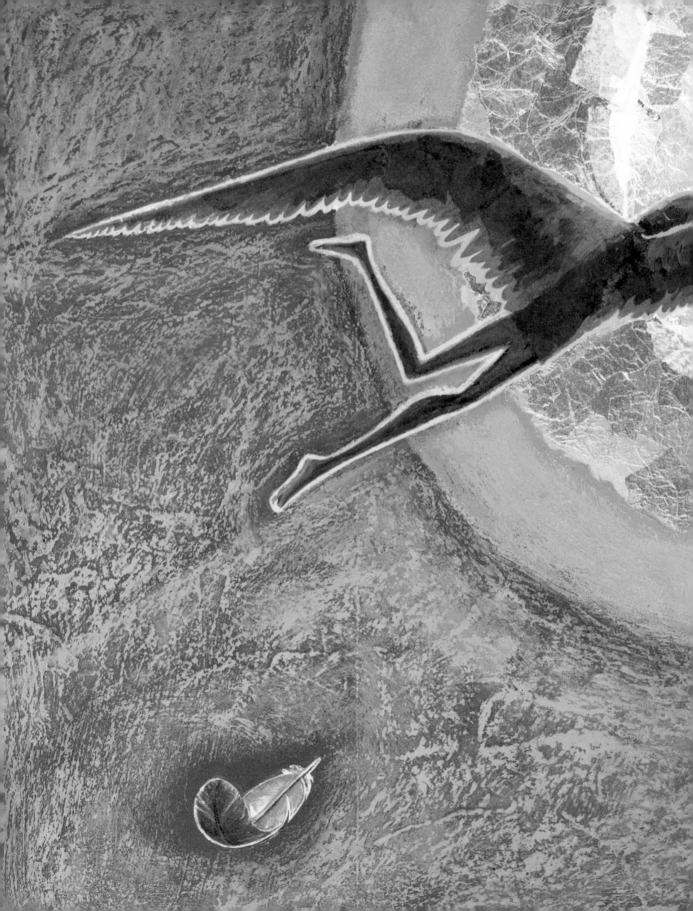

Higher and higher flew Icarus, towards the strengthening sun. The air grew hotter, the sun more brilliant, dazzling to his eyes. He had forgotten all warnings now, flying nearer as if drawn to it, like a moth towards a lamp.

And slowly the wax on his wings began to melt. It softened gently, then dripped a little, in slow, thick drops. A feather slipped from it, fell drifting, turning, down towards the sea. Other feathers followed, singly at first, but then more and more of them at once. And suddenly, though the ecstatic Icarus as confidently moved his wings, there were not enough feathers left to hold the air, to keep him up in flight.

His father looked back, to see his son plunge headlong, faster than the feathers, passing every one. Straight as a gull he fell towards the sea, but did not swerve in safety like a gull above the glittering waves. He plunged right into the heart of them, and their startled waters closed above his head. All that remained of Icarus were some feathers floating on the sea, while his father flew, weeping, in the sky, alone.